Maps AND Mapping

MAPPING

MONEY AND TRADE

BY
MADELINE TYLER

KidHaven
PUBLISHING

Published in 2020 by KidHaven Publishing, an Imprint of Greenhaven Publishing, LLC
353 3rd Avenue, Suite 255, New York, NY 10010

Written by: Madeline Tyler
Edited by: Kirsty Holmes
Designed by: Drue Rintoul

Cataloging-in-Publication Data

Names: Tyler, Madeline.
Title: Mapping money and trade / Madeline Tyler.
Description: New York : KidHaven Publishing, 2020. | Series: Maps and mapping | Includes glossary.
Identifiers: ISBN 9781534531123 (pbk.) | ISBN 9781534530232 (library bound) | ISBN 9781534531536 (6 pack) | ISBN 9781534531062 (ebook)
Subjects: LCSH: International trade--History--Juvenile literature. | Globalization--Economic aspects--Juvenile literature. |
Economic geography--Maps--Juvenile literature.
Classification: LCC HF1379.T95 2020 | DDC 382'.09--dc23

Image Credits
All images are courtesy of Shutterstock.com, unless otherwise specified. With thanks to Getty Images, Thinkstock Photo and iStockphoto.
Front Cover – Pigprox, vinnstock. 2 – tcly. 4&5 – Shpadaruk Aleksei, Rainer Lesniewski, D1min, Andy Vinnikov. 6&7 – quangmooo, Max3105, Julia Tim, Mahesh Patil. 8&9
– Cvijovic Zarko, Vanatchanan. 10&11 – ashva, Rvector, tonynetone (via Flickr.com), By Brianann MacAmhlaidh (Own work) [CC BY-SA 4.0 (https://creativecommons.org/
licenses/by-sa/4.0), via Wikimedia Commons. 12&13 – Peter Hermes Furia, Richard Cavalleri. 14&15 – By Viajes_de_colon.svg: Phirosiberia derivative work: Phirosiberia
(Viajes_de_colon.svg) [CC BY-SA 3.0 (https://creativecommons.org/licenses/by-sa/3.0) or GFDL (http://www.gnu.org/copyleft/fdl.html)], via Wikimedia Commons.
16&17 – By Evan T Jones (Own work) [CC BY-SA 4.0 (https://creativecommons.org/licenses/by-sa/4.0), via Wikimedia Commons, Karte: NordNordWest, Lizenz: Creative
Commons by-sa-3.0 de [CC BY-SA 3.0 de (https://creativecommons.org/licenses/by-sa/3.0/de/deed.en)], via Wikimedia Commons. 18&19 – Evannovostro, Galina Savina,
pavalena. 20&21 – B.S. Halpern (T. Hengl; D. Groll) / Wikimedia Commons, via Wikimedia Commons, tcly, Nighlman1965, By Jpatokal (Own work) [CC BY-SA 3.0 (https://
creativecommons.org/licenses/by-sa/3.0) or GFDL (http://www.gnu.org/copyleft/fdl.html)], via Wikimedia Commons. 22&23 – Sean, By Ali Zifan (Own work; Used a
blank map from here.) [CC0], via Wikimedia Commons. 24&25 – T. Lesia, By Original PNG : User:Bernese media, User:BIL 2011 SVG version: User:Akwa and others (see
source file) [CC BY-SA 3.0 (https://creativecommons.org/licenses/by-sa/3.0)], via Wikimedia Commons, RidwanFadilArif at English Wikipedia [GFDL (http://www.gnu.org/
copyleft/fdl.html) or CC BY-SA 3.0 (https://creativecommons.org/licenses/by-sa/3.0)], via Wikimedia Commons. 26&27 – vipman, User:Tony0106 [CC BY-SA 3.0 (https://
creativecommons.org/licenses/by-sa/3.0) or GFDL (http://www.gnu.org/copyleft/fdl.html)], via Wikimedia Commons, By M Tracy Hunter (Own work) [CC BY-SA 3.0 (https://
creativecommons.org/licenses/by-sa/3.0)], via Wikimedia Commons, Donatas Dabravolskas. 28&29 – By Redgeographics (Created map from scratch) [GFDL (http://
www.gnu.org/copyleft/fdl.html) or CC BY-SA 4.0 (https://creativecommons.org/licenses/by-sa/4.0), via Wikimedia Commons, Ake13bk, By ThoughtIdRetired [CC BY-SA 3.0
(https://creativecommons.org/licenses/by-sa/3.0)], via Wikimedia Commons. 30 – Thinglass, pingebat.

Printed in the United States of America

CPSIA compliance information: Batch #BS19KL: For further information contact Greenhaven Publishing LLC, New York, New York at 1-844-317-7404.

CONTENTS

Words that look like **this** are explained in the glossary on page 31.

WHAT ARE MAPS FOR?

What Is a Map?

Maps are **diagrams** that show parts of the world and how they are connected. Maps can show a big area, like the entire world, or a small area, like a village or woodland. Some maps only show natural **features** of the landscape, like mountains and rivers. Other maps show where buildings and roads are. Some maps only show specific things, like amusement park maps, which are for visitors to find their way around the park and plan their day.

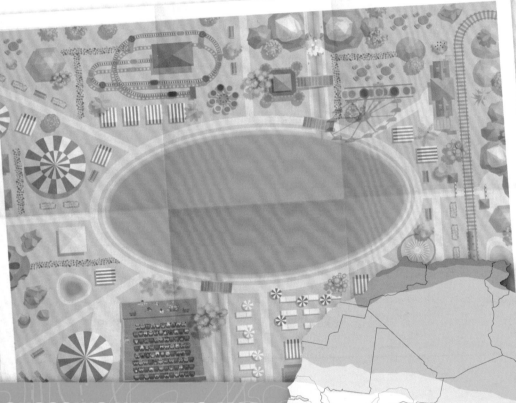

With this map, a visitor can see where all the rides and roller coasters are and how to get to each one.

CHOOSING WHAT TO MAP

A mapmaker, called a cartographer, often can't put all parts of an area on a map. Because some things are left out, or simplified, a map doesn't always look exactly like a place. It is a drawing instead of a photo. Maps are useful to see certain features, **landmarks**, people, vegetation, or animals. The finished map can show some of these things clearly, but can't show everything, so they have to choose what is important.

BY NOT INCLUDING OTHER INFORMATION, THE MAP OF AFRICA IS EASIER TO READ.

This map of Africa only shows some natural features, like vegetation, and not towns or cities.

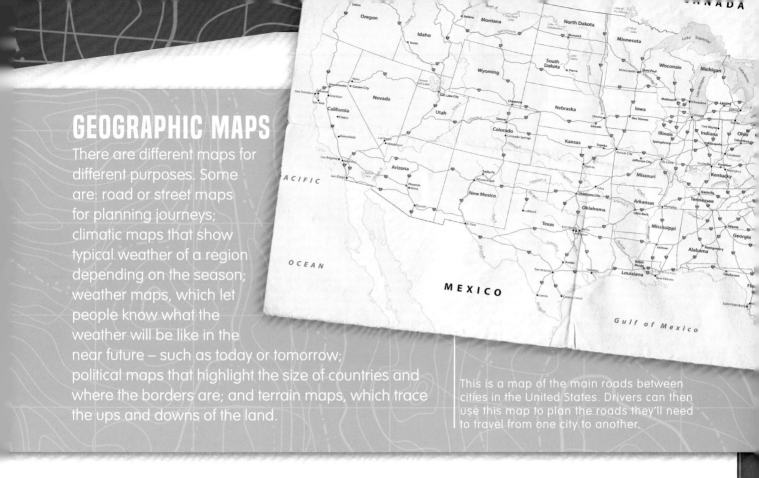

GEOGRAPHIC MAPS

There are different maps for different purposes. Some are: road or street maps for planning journeys; climatic maps that show typical weather of a region depending on the season; weather maps, which let people know what the weather will be like in the near future – such as today or tomorrow; political maps that highlight the size of countries and where the borders are; and terrain maps, which trace the ups and downs of the land.

This is a map of the main roads between cities in the United States. Drivers can then use this map to plan the roads they'll need to travel from one city to another.

Non-Geographic Maps

There are even maps of objects and other things that aren't on the surface of the Earth. There are maps of space, such as solar system maps. There are tree maps that show the order that things happened and how they are linked. For example, a family tree is an easy way to see how everyone in a family is related. Mind maps are ways to come up with ideas that are linked to one main topic.

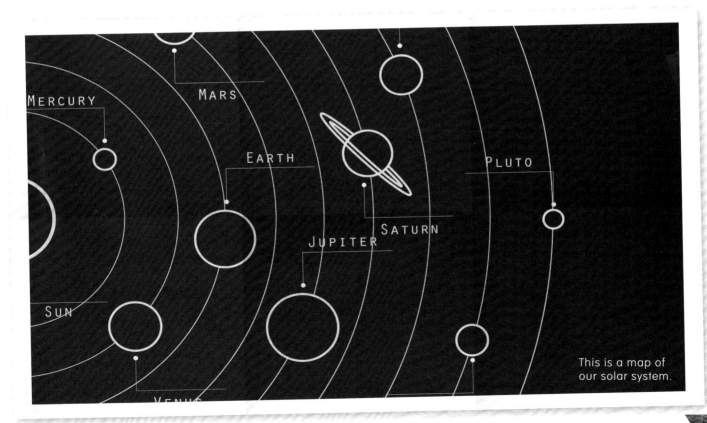

This is a map of our solar system.

WHAT ARE
MONEY AND TRADE?

What Is Trade?

Trade is another way of describing swapping or exchanging things. People have always needed to trade things with other people so they can have all the different things they need. For example, someone with a lot of food might be able to trade some of that food, and swap it with someone who had a lot of cloth for making clothes. Then everyone will have the things they need. Countries can trade, too – a country with a lot of **fossil fuels** might trade with a country that produces a lot of wood.

Wood, also called lumber, is a natural material that countries trade.

WHAT IS MONEY?

Money is another word for a system of notes and tokens or coins that can be swapped for any other kind of goods or services. Before money was invented, people only traded goods. Someone might have swapped some chickens for some cloth. But not everyone would want your chickens, so you might find it hard to trade. Money can be swapped for anything, so trade becomes easier.

Money comes in coins and notes. Different countries have different money systems. These are called currencies.

KEY TERMS

Goods: Products you can buy, sell, or trade

Services: When someone's time or actions are bought or traded, for example a builder

Credit: When someone allows you to buy something and pay for it later

Debit: Taking money directly from someone's account

Bank Account: Where the bank stores and counts your money

Market: The place where trading is done – small markets in a town or large, international markets

WHO CAN TRADE?

A trade takes place whenever someone exchanges a product or service for a payment of some kind. Trades can happen between individual people, companies, or countries. If you buy one chocolate bar from a shop, this is an example of trade. A large company ordering 1,000 chocolate bars from a factory or a **supplier** is also a trade – trades can be big or small.

UK
Home Market

International
Trade

UK Foreign
Market

Trading Across Borders

All companies have to be registered somewhere, even big companies that trade and do business with many different countries.

The country that they are registered and based in is their domestic, or home, market and all other countries are their foreign market. A chocolate factory in the United Kingdom might trade with a foreign market like Spain by selling chocolate to different shops in the country. Trade between the UK and Spain is an example of international trade. International trade can be mapped between several countries, and from one country to many others.

What Are Imports?

Sometimes, a country does not make enough of a product, or they do not have the right **resources** to make the product at all. When this happens, the country can bring the product in from abroad and sell it in their country. This is called importing, and the products are called imports.

This map shows where countries in the Americas import most of their products from.

MAPPING IMPORTS

Different countries import different materials, resources, or products. Some countries have plenty of fuel but no cars, while other countries might have lots of food, but no electronics.

The biggest imports of each country in the Americas are shown on this map.

Key

Fuel
Food and Produce
Transportation

WHAT ARE EXPORTS?

Some countries make so much of a particular product that they can sell it to other countries for a **profit**. When a country sells products to another country, it is called exporting.

Have you ever looked at a toy or a piece of electronic equipment such as a smartphone and seen a label that says "Made in China?" This means that the product was **manufactured** in China and then exported abroad.

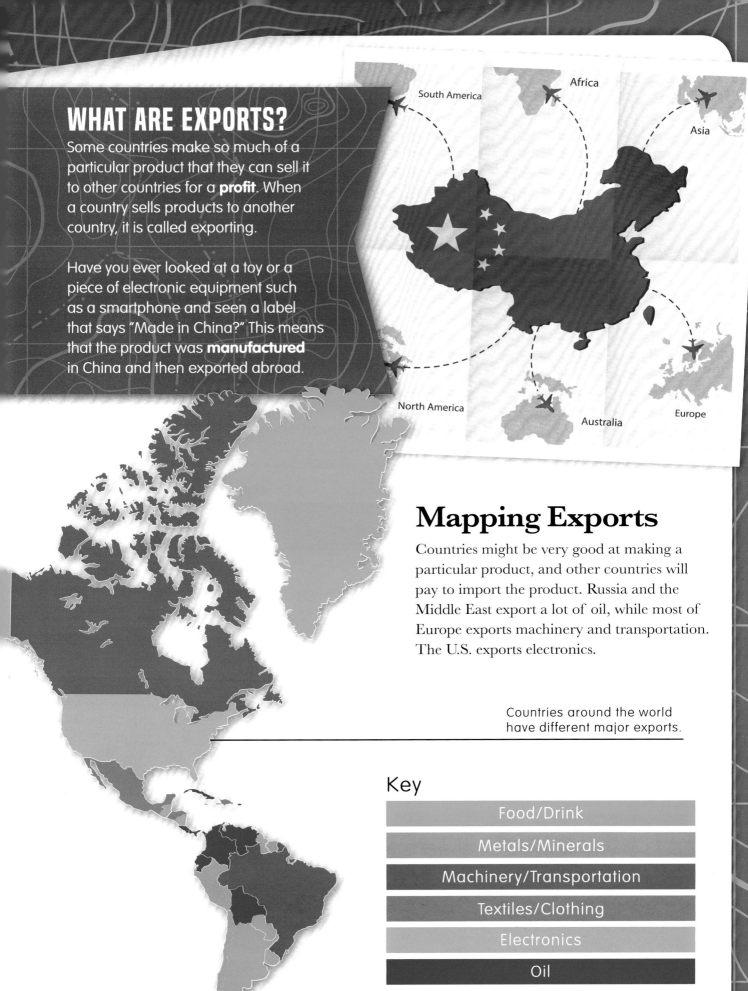

Mapping Exports

Countries might be very good at making a particular product, and other countries will pay to import the product. Russia and the Middle East export a lot of oil, while most of Europe exports machinery and transportation. The U.S. exports electronics.

Countries around the world have different major exports.

Key

Food/Drink
Metals/Minerals
Machinery/Transportation
Textiles/Clothing
Electronics
Oil

EARLY TRADERS

Ancient Trading

People have been trading goods and services for thousands of years, even before modern money was created. Early types of trade were called bartering and involved exchanging one service or item for another, without using money. Bartering dates back around 8,000 years to **Mesopotamia**, when people exchanged goods for things like food, tea, and spices. Many things had a different value than what they have now: one example is salt. Salt was worth so much that part of the Roman soldiers' salaries were made up of it!

SALT

THE WORD "SALARY" COMES FROM THE LATIN WORD FOR SALT: SAL.

THE SILK ROAD

The Silk Road was a network of trading routes thousands of years ago that started in China and connected the rest of Asia with Europe. **Merchants** would travel along the land and sea routes, transporting various **commodities** to be exchanged with other traders. Although silk was the first product to be sold along this route, it became a major trade route for textiles, spices, grains, fruit, and art.

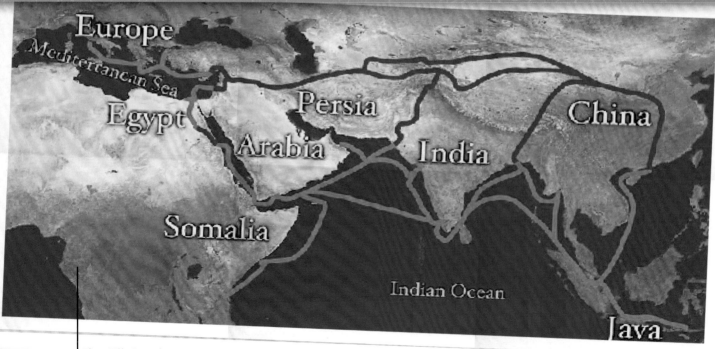

Europe
Mediterranean Sea
Egypt
Persia
Arabia
India
China
Somalia
Indian Ocean
Java

The Silk Road

THE VIKINGS

The Vikings were a group of people from **Scandinavia** who traveled the sea in their longboats, raiding and invading many settlements in Europe. The Vikings started in Denmark, Sweden, and Norway, and traveled as far as North America to start new settlements for themselves.

Although the Vikings have a reputation of being fierce warriors, many Vikings were not very fearsome. Many traveled to new lands to live and work as farmers, craftsmen, or traders.

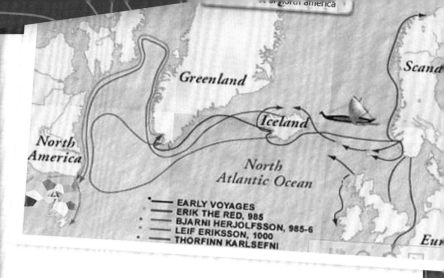

Viking Traders

The Vikings had many commodities, but there were some products that they could not find or make in their homelands. They exported goods such as bear and beaver fur, bedding stuffed with feathers, and weapons in exchange for spices from the Middle East, silk from Turkey and China, and wine from France and Germany. They carried the imports and exports in large boats called merchant ships.

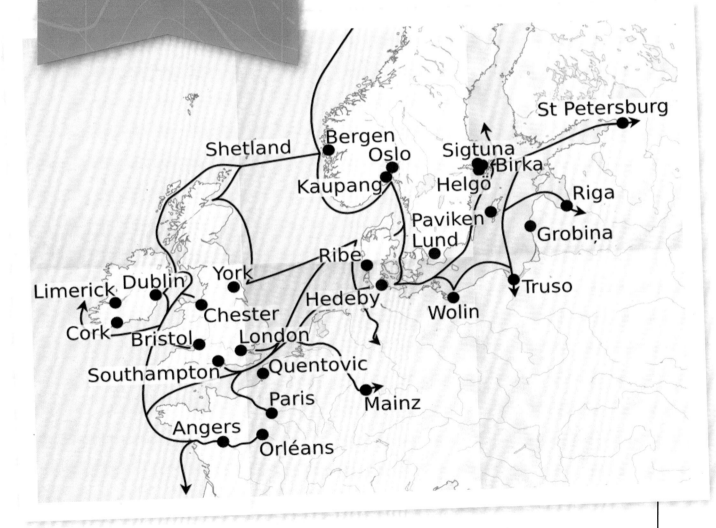

The Vikings' trade routes helped to develop Europe's economy.

Getting Around Africa

Bartolomeu Dias was a Portuguese explorer in the late 15th century. In 1487, King John II of Portugal sent Dias to find a trade route to India by sea. Portugal and other European countries already had trade routes to Asia, but all of these were on land. The land routes were taken under control by the **Ottoman Empire** in the 1450s, so European traders had to find new ways of reaching Asia. Explorers could either sail east around Africa, or west into the unknown Atlantic Ocean.

Dias chose to sail east and, in 1488, he became the first European to sail around the Cape of Good Hope, the most southwesterly point of Africa. Although Dias never reached India, his journey made it possible for future explorers to travel further.

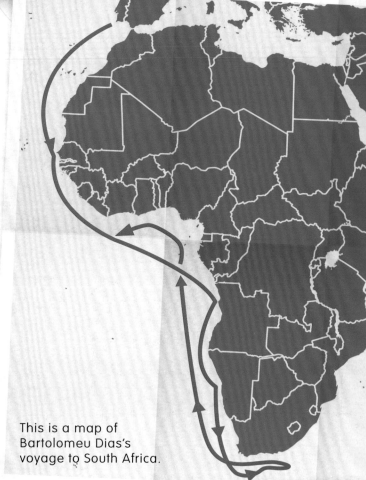

This is a map of Bartolomeu Dias's voyage to South Africa.

The Cape of Good Hope was originally called the Cape of Storms by Dias because of the bad weather that made it so difficult to navigate around the cape.

REACHING INDIA

When Dias returned to Portugal, he was asked by the king to help design a new ship for another Portuguese **expedition**, also headed for India. The expedition was led by a captain called Vasco da Gama, an explorer who learned to sail and **navigate** in the Portuguese navy.

In 1497, nine years after Dias's voyage, da Gama set off to reach India by sea. By following Dias's route down the West African coast to the Cape of Good Hope, he eventually succeeded and became the first European to sail to India. Da Gama landed in Calicut (now Kozhikode) on May 20, 1498.

Portugal was then able to export spices such as pepper and cinnamon out of India and sell them to the European market. Portugal had a **monopoly** of Indian exports for many years until other European countries challenged Portugal by sailing to India.

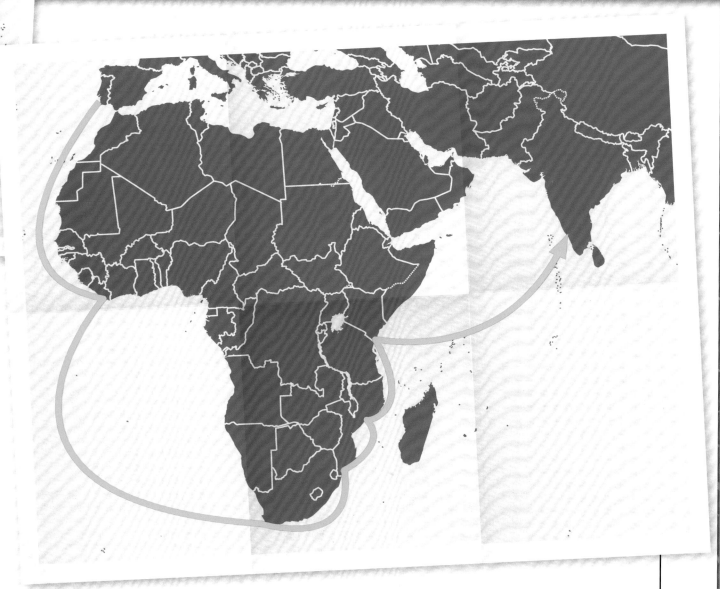

The discovery of this route transformed European and Asian trade. European sailors began using it, and the first Portuguese trading post was soon established in India.

FINDING THE AMERICAS

Landing in the Americas

Christopher Columbus was an Italian explorer in the 15th century. In 1492, King Ferdinand and Queen Isabella of Spain gave Columbus a lot of money to find a new trade route to Asia by sailing west instead of the usual east. Because maps of the time made the oceans look much smaller, Columbus hoped to reach India, China and the East Indies in just a few days. However, the Atlantic Ocean, which separates Europe and the Americas, is actually the second-largest ocean in the world, so the voyage took them much longer. Columbus and his crew were traveling for 36 days before they eventually spotted land.

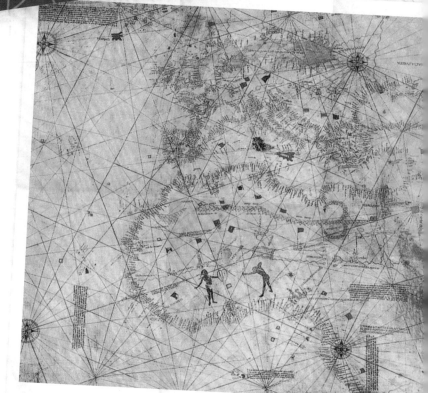

This map shows how people in 1490 saw the world.

Columbus traveled to the Caribbean islands four times.

When Columbus landed, he believed he had reached the East Indies. The islands he found were actually in the Bahamas and the Caribbean, just off the coast of Central America, and were mostly unknown to the rest of the world until that point.

ATLANTIC OCEAN

PACIFIC OCEAN

Florida
The Bahamas
Habana
Cuba
Santo Domingo
Yucatán
Jamaica
CENTRAL AMERICA
Guadeloupe
Martinique
Colón
Panamá
Maracaibo
Coro
Caracas
Cumaná

Azores Islands
Lisbon
PORTUGAL
SPA
Madeira
Canary Islands

Cape Verde

AFRICA

SOUTH AMERICA

Galápagos Islands

First voyage
Second voyage
Third voyage
Fourth voyage

NAMING THE AMERICAS

Amerigo Vespucci was an Italian explorer, like Christopher Columbus. Around the year 1500, eight years after Columbus first sailed to the Americas, Vespucci traveled to the "New World." Unlike Columbus, Vespucci was convinced that the lands were part of a new continent, and not part of Asia. Vespucci wrote down all his findings to share with the rest of the world.

Amerigo Vespucci explored lots of Central and South America.

Not long after, new maps had to be created to show the new landmass. In the early 16th century, cartographers Matthias Ringmann and Martin Waldseemuller used Vespucci's notes to create a new world map. This was one of the first maps to include the lands explored by Columbus and Vespucci and was the first place where it was named America. Many people believe that Ringmann and Waldseemuller named America after Amerigo Vespucci to celebrate his discovery that it was separate from Asia.

Ringmann and Waldseemuller's Map, 1507

Landing in Canada

The 15th and 16th centuries are sometimes known as the Age of Discovery because, while competing to find new routes to Asia, many European countries were accidentally discovering new lands to explore. Asian countries, like China and India, were very important trading partners during this time because they exported commodities that were not available in Europe, like spices, perfumes, and silk.

This painting from the 12th century shows women in China inspecting some silk.

John Cabot, also called Giovanni Caboto, was an explorer and navigator from Venice, Italy, during the Age of Discovery. Like many explorers before him, Cabot also wanted to try and discover a new and shorter trade route to Asia. In 1497, Cabot left Bristol on behalf of King Henry VII of England to sail west. Around a month into his journey, Cabot saw Canadian land and named it New-found-land. Cabot became the first European explorer to reach mainland North America since the Vikings in the 11th century.

No one is sure exactly where Cabot first landed in Canada, but it could be Newfoundland, Cape Breton Island, or southern Labrador.

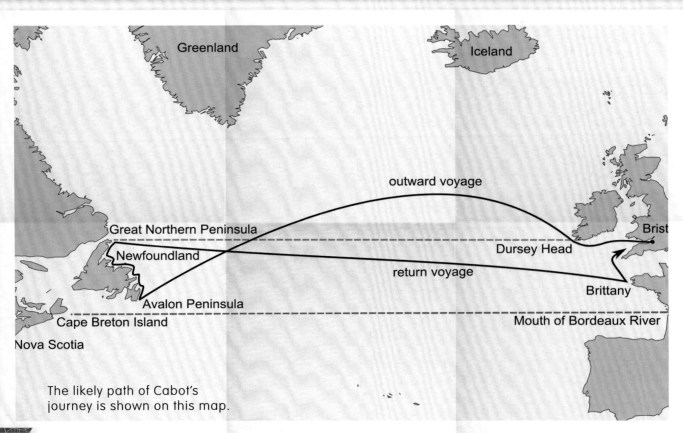

The likely path of Cabot's journey is shown on this map.

MAPPING THE AMERICAS

Juan de la Cosa was a Spanish explorer and cartographer who sailed with Christopher Columbus on his first three journeys to the Americas, and with Amerigo Vespucci and Alonso de Ojeda to Central and South America. Alonso de Ojeda was a Spanish navigator who led an expedition in 1499 to the South American mainland. Vespucci, de la Cosa, and de Ojeda became some of the first people from Europe to set foot on the mainland of South America. They explored the Gulf of Paria, Cape Vela (Cabo de la Vela), and the Essequibo River.

During his voyage with Vespucci and de Ojeda, de la Cosa spent lots of his time carefully mapping all of the places he explored. On his return to Europe in 1500, de la Cosa produced a world map called the Mappa Mundi. This is the first European map to include the new lands on the other side of the Atlantic Ocean.

This is a German map of the Gulf of Paria, between Venezuela and Trinidad and Tobago.

The islands of Cuba and Hispaniola can be seen on this map.

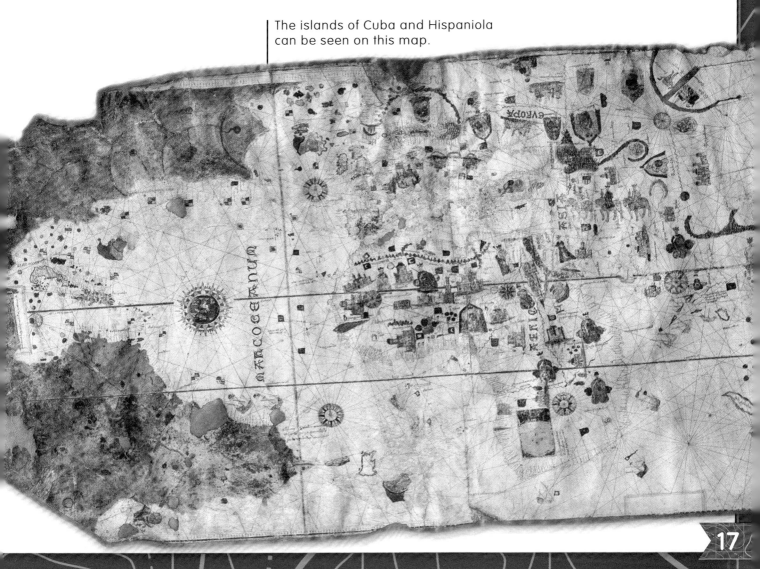

Suez Canal

A canal is a waterway made by people, like an artificial river, usually built and used for travel and trade. The Suez Canal was first opened in 1869 and is thought to be the world's first artificial waterway used for transporting goods and people. The Suez Canal is 101 miles (163 km) long and connects the Mediterranean Sea with the Red Sea. It is the fastest way to reach the Indian Ocean from the Atlantic Ocean and transformed trade and travel because people in Europe no longer had to travel around Africa to reach Asia.

When the Suez Canal was first opened, it could only take ships that weighed up to a maximum of 5,510 tons (5,000 t). The canal was recently widened and lengthened and, in 2015, nearly 17,500 ships passed through it. It is now one of the busiest shipping lanes in the world.

It takes between 11 and 16 hours for a ship to pass through the Suez Canal.

Panama Canal

In 1513, a Spanish explorer called Vasco Núñez de Balboa found a crossing between the Atlantic and Pacific Oceans while looking for gold in Panama. During his time in Central America, de Balboa crossed the **Isthmus** of Panama and spotted the Atlantic Ocean to the east and the Pacific Ocean to the west. However, despite de Balboa's finding, it was many hundreds of years before any work began on building a canal in the area.

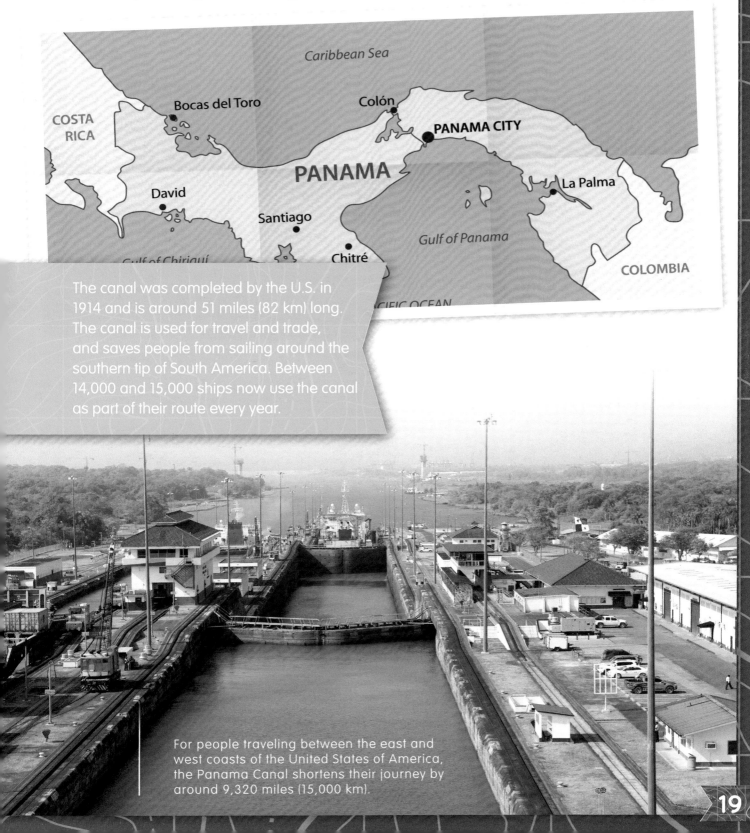

Caribbean Sea

Bocas del Toro

Colón

PANAMA CITY

COSTA RICA

PANAMA

David

La Palma

Santiago

Gulf of Panama

Chitré

Gulf of Chiriquí

COLOMBIA

PACIFIC OCEAN

The canal was completed by the U.S. in 1914 and is around 51 miles (82 km) long. The canal is used for travel and trade, and saves people from sailing around the southern tip of South America. Between 14,000 and 15,000 ships now use the canal as part of their route every year.

For people traveling between the east and west coasts of the United States of America, the Panama Canal shortens their journey by around 9,320 miles (15,000 km).

Goods on the Move

With the discoveries of new trade routes and the creation of new canals, trade between different countries grew. Trucks, planes and ships are constantly on the move, transporting **cargo** by land, air, and sea between the countries. Cargo ships are the busiest as they carry 90% of all world trade.

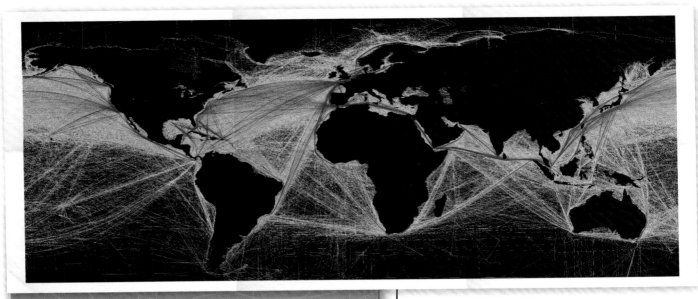

More than 50,000 ships transport cargo around the world. This map shows their routes.

Different ships are needed to carry different goods.

- Around 17,000 of the 50,000 ships are bulk carriers. These ships carry a lot of one type of product, like coal or grain.
- Around 11,000 are general cargo ships. These carry trees, vehicles, machinery, steel, and food products.
- 11,000 are oil tankers that only transport oil.
- Only around 7,000 are container ships.

Container Ship

THE LARGEST CONTAINER PORT IN THE WORLD IS IN SHANGHAI, CHINA. AROUND 30 MILLION CONTAINERS PASS THROUGH IT EVERY YEAR.

PLANES

Planes carry less than 1% of all world trade, but the goods they carry are worth 35% of the total **value** of trade worldwide. Planes are much faster than ships and only take around 10 days to deliver an item, instead of 70 days for a ship. Goods delivered by plane usually need to be delivered more urgently and are mostly computers, machinery, and electrical equipment.

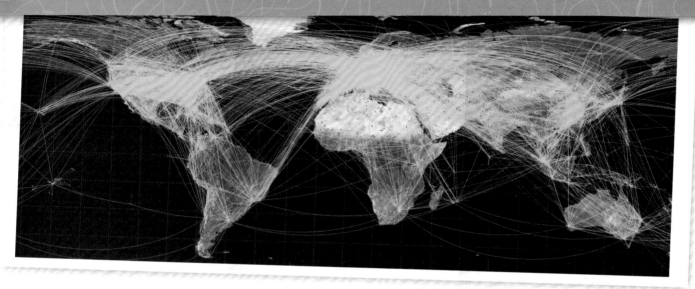

Trucks

When cargo arrives at a port or airport, it needs to be moved to its next destination, and this is usually done by large trucks. Container ships carry containers that are all standard sizes. This means that they can easily be loaded straight from the ships onto the back of a truck.

IN THE U.S., MORE THAN 70% OF ALL BULK GOODS ARE TRANSPORTED BY TRUCK.

MAPPING
THE ECONOMY

What Is the Economy?

The economy is how money is made and used within a country. A country's economy is related to what products and services it imports and exports, and also how much money people spend on these things. Economies are very different across the world. One way they are studied and measured is by looking at the gross domestic product (GDP) of each country.

GROSS DOMESTIC PRODUCT

Gross domestic product is something that people can use to measure the economy and wealth of a country.

- Gross means the total of something.
- Domestic means national, as opposed to international. This means that the GDP only refers to one country.
- Product is another word for goods or services.

The GDP of a country is the amount of money it makes in a set amount of time, usually a year. To calculate the GDP, you must add together all the money a country makes from things like exporting products. Then you need to subtract (take away) all the money that the country spends on making and importing goods.

Nominal GDP in Billion U.S. Dollar

5000 $
1000 $
500 $
100 $
50 $
20 $
1 $
No Data

Countries by GDP (Nominal) in 2014

This map of the world shows which countries had the highest and lowest GDP in 2014.

GDP PER CAPITA

Not all countries are the same size. Some countries are very big, like Russia, while others are very small, like Singapore. As well as this, not all countries have the same population, or amount of people, living there. So, even if a country has a high GDP, it may need to be shared between more people.

To find out how GDP affects the people in a country, it is useful to divide the GDP by the number of people living in that country. This gives a number called the GDP per capita, or GDP per person, which is the average amount of money available to each person in the country.

THIS MAP SHOWS COUNTRIES SIZED ACCORDING TO GDP. COUNTRIES WITH A HIGH GDP ARE SHOWN BIGGER THAN COUNTRIES WITH A SMALL GDP.

By looking at the GDP per capita, we can measure people's quality of life in these countries. A high GDP per capita means that the average person has quite a lot of money whereas a low GDP per capita means that they do not have much money.

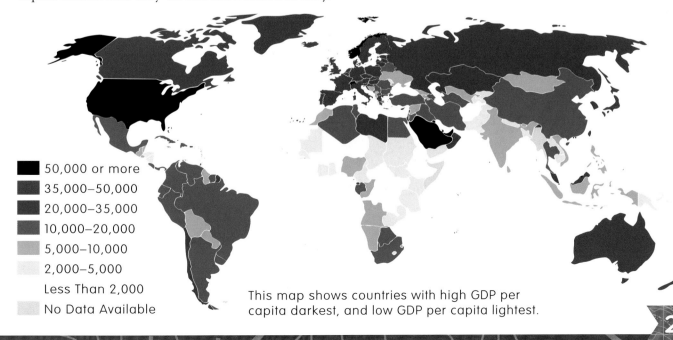

- 50,000 or more
- 35,000–50,000
- 20,000–35,000
- 10,000–20,000
- 5,000–10,000
- 2,000–5,000
- Less Than 2,000
- No Data Available

This map shows countries with high GDP per capita darkest, and low GDP per capita lightest.

More Economically Developed Countries

Countries are usually said to be either more economically developed countries (MEDCs) or less economically developed countries (LEDCs). Different things are measured to decide which category a country should be in. Some examples of these include: how many schools and hospitals there are, how many roads and train tracks cover the country, and how much access they have to electricity.

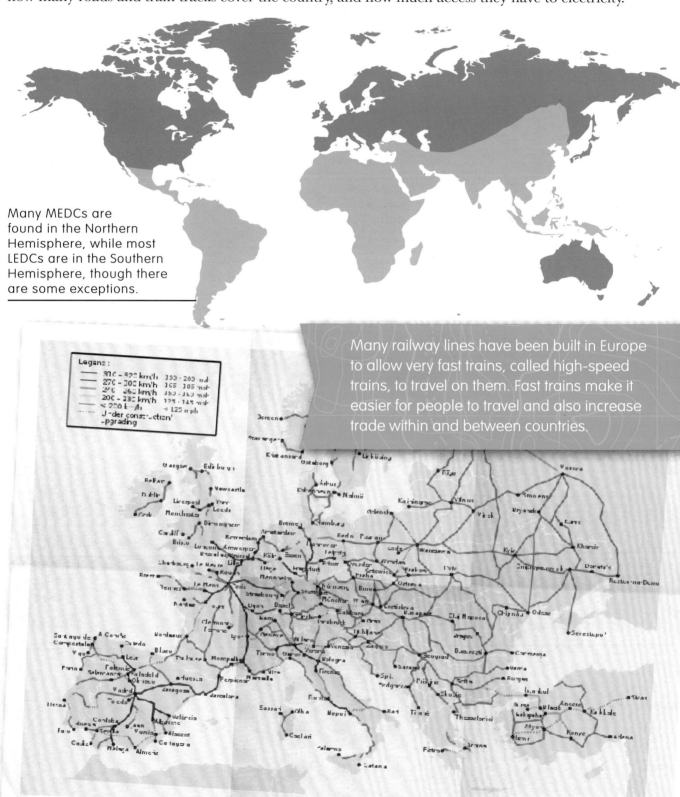

Many MEDCs are found in the Northern Hemisphere, while most LEDCs are in the Southern Hemisphere, though there are some exceptions.

Many railway lines have been built in Europe to allow very fast trains, called high-speed trains, to travel on them. Fast trains make it easier for people to travel and also increase trade within and between countries.

This map of Europe shows the railway lines for high-speed trains.

LESS ECONOMICALLY DEVELOPED COUNTRIES

Some countries may have fewer schools, hospitals, and roads. There may also not be enough trains to take people to work, or enough electricity to provide light and warmth in everyone's homes. These are called less economically developed countries.

This is a map of the world at night that was taken from space.
The white spots are lights, which are powered by electricity.
LEDCs and areas with a low population will look darker on this map.

Newly Industrialized Countries

Many countries fall somewhere between being less economically developed and more economically developed; these countries are called developing or newly **industrialized** countries. Newly industrialized countries have larger economies than LEDCs, but the people may have lower life expectancies and less education than people in MEDCs.

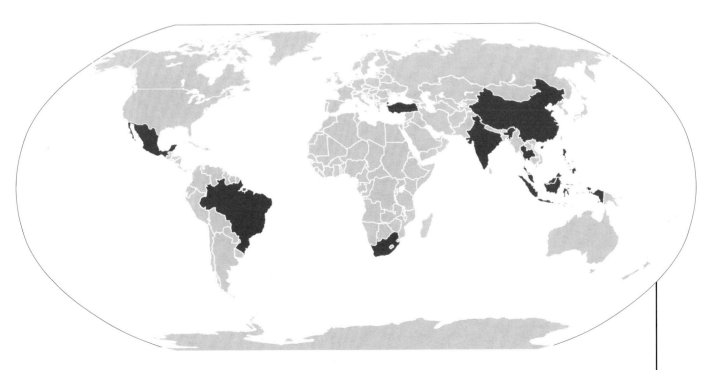

Mexico, Brazil, South Africa, India, and China are considered to be newly industrialized countries.

25

MAPPING WEALTH

Wealth Distribution and Wealth Inequality

GDP per capita is how much money each person living in a country would have if the country's money was shared equally amongst everyone. However, this is not what happens in real life. People have different jobs and earn different **wages** – some people have a lot more money than the GDP per capita, and some people have a lot less.

Wealth means how much money a person or a country has. If someone has a high amount of wealth, they are rich, or wealthy, and if someone has a low amount they might be called poor, or said to be living in poverty.

The difference between the rich and the poor in a society is called wealth inequality. It is a measure of how unequally the wealth of a country is distributed, or shared, between its citizens. Wealth inequality is measured by looking at how much people earn in their wages, how much money they have in savings, and how much their possessions are worth.

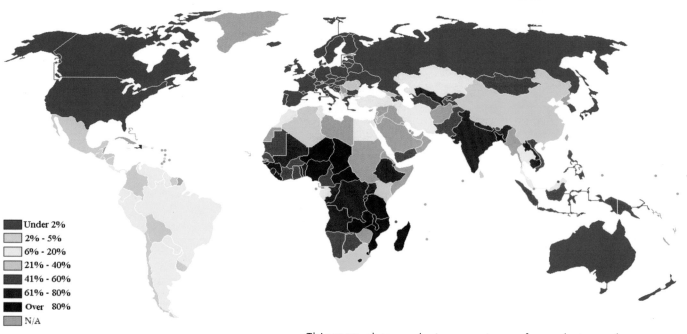

Under 2%
2% - 5%
6% - 20%
21% - 40%
41% - 60%
61% - 80%
Over 80%
N/A

This map shows what percentage of people in each country were living on less than $2 a day in 2009.

INCOME INEQUALITY

If everyone in a country earned exactly the same as each other, the country would have perfect income equality. However, if some of the population earn a lot of money and others earn very little, then the country's income inequality would be very high.

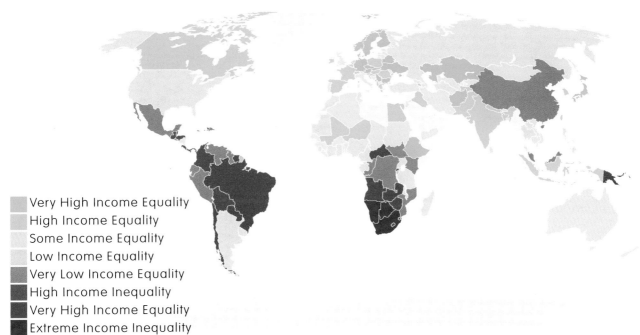

- Very High Income Equality
- High Income Equality
- Some Income Equality
- Low Income Equality
- Very Low Income Equality
- High Income Inequality
- Very High Income Equality
- Extreme Income Inequality

This is a map of income inequality around the world.

Wealth and Income Inequality in Brazil

Although Brazil has one of the largest economies in the world, it also has one of the highest rates of wealth inequality. Inequality in Brazil is so high that it would take someone earning the minimum monthly wage 19 years to earn what one of the richest people in Brazil makes in one month.

Favela de Rocinha, the biggest slum in Brazil, is next to Rio de Janeiro.

CASE STUDY: MAPPING TEA

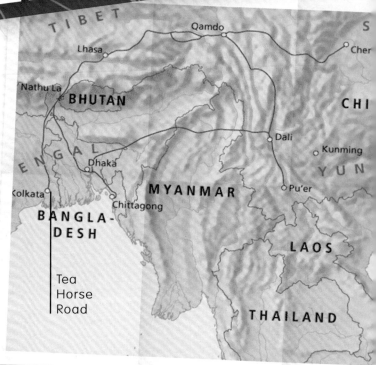

Tea and Horses

Tea has been grown in China for thousands of years and, in the 10th century, it became a very important and valuable export. People in China started trading tea with people in Tibet in exchange for horses. The Chinese traders would transport the tea almost 1,400 miles (2,250 km) from where the tea was grown to Lhasa, the capital of Tibet. The journey was very dangerous and took the traders around three months to complete. It is because of these exchanges that the route became known as the Tea Horse Road.

TEA IN INDIA

Hundreds of years later, tea was brought to Europe. A British trading company called the East India Company started trading wool from Britain and cotton from India for Chinese tea. Eventually, the East India Company began growing tea in India and, by 1888, more tea was grown in India than in China and they soon had a monopoly on all tea trade in the UK.

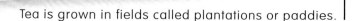
Tea is grown in fields called plantations or paddies.

TEA EXPORTS

India still grows and exports a lot of tea, but many countries now export a lot more. Although countries like Kenya, India, and Turkey export a lot of tea, China and Sri Lanka export and sell their tea at a much higher price – this means they actually make more money from their tea and make a higher profit.

From 0.5 to 1%
From 1% to 5%
From 5% to 10%
From 10% to 20%
More than 20%

The countries that produce the most tea are shown on this map.

Tea Imports

In the 19th century, tea had to be brought from India and China in very large sailing ships, called clippers. They had to sail all the way around Africa, so the journey often took more than three months to complete. Now, however, tea can be transported across the world much quicker because of the Suez Canal, airplanes, and faster ships.

Every year, around $6 **billion** is spent across the world on importing tea. In 2016, Russia imported the most tea and spent $548.3 million, over $100 million more than the United Kingdom paid!

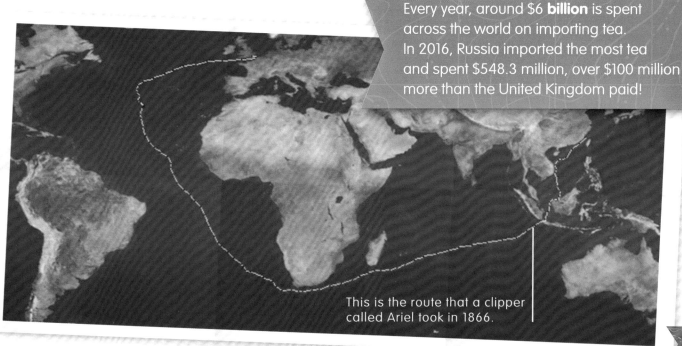

This is the route that a clipper called Ariel took in 1866.

FAIR TRADE

In most MEDCs, there are rules and regulations that make sure businesses treat their workers fairly. The rules tell the businesses how much they must pay their workers, when the workers must be allowed to take a break, and how many hours they can work in one shift. In lots of LEDCs, these rules do not exist: the workers often receive low wages and are treated unfairly.

Fair trade is a movement that wants farmers and workers in LEDCs to get a fair deal. Fair trade is trying to ensure that all workers receive a fair wage and work under reasonable conditions. These people can then use the money to feed their families and even send their children to school. Fair trade works in 74 countries and helps 1.65 million farmers and workers in 1,226 different organizations.

Some popular fair trade products include bananas, chocolate, coffee, sugar, and tea.

Fair trade producer countries

Fair trade consumer countries

abroad	in another country
billion	one thousand million
cargo	items usually carried on ships, including cattle, food, tools, and furniture
commodities	materials or products that can be bought and sold
diagrams	simplified drawings that show the appearance, structure, or workings of something
expedition	a journey for a specific purpose
features	distinctive properties of the landscape, i.e. not flat
fossil fuels	fuels, such as coal, oil, and gas, that formed millions of years ago from the remains of animals and plants
industrialized	to make industrial; if a country makes goods and services in large factories, it is industrial
isthmus	a narrow strip of land that connects two larger pieces of land
landmarks	parts of the landscape that can be used as reference points
manufactured	to make a large quantity of something
merchants	people involved in trading goods, often with other countries
Mesopotamia	a settlement in the ancient Middle East
monopoly	complete control over a product or service in a specific area
navigate	find a route, or chart a course for a ship
Ottoman Empire	a Turkish empire that was founded in the 14th century
profit	the amount of money that a company makes that is more than the amount paid in expenses
resources	supplies of money, materials, and people
Scandinavia	a region in northern Europe made up of Norway, Sweden, Denmark, and Finland
supplier	a company that sells products
value	the worth of something
wages	money paid to a person for the work they do

INDEX